THE LANGUAGE
OF HANDWRITING

THE
LANGUAGE
OF
HANDWRITING

and

how to read it

•

BY

OSCAR N. MYER

•

An easy-to-use guide
to handwriting analysis
with 70 tables and
350 handwriting samples

STEPHEN DAYE PRESS
NEW YORK

CONTENTS

CONTENTS

INTRODUCTION

The following tables are, first of all, an attempt to list the principal features of graphology. The purpose of handwriting analysis is to ascertain the character of people through the medium of their handwriting.

It is quite natural that we should try to size up the people we meet; we want to find out about their personality and character, and as long as we encounter frankness and sincerity this should not be too hard. If, on the other hand, we are faced with secretiveness, our judgment may be inadequate or even wrong. Modern psychology has developed many methods, including tests, the purpose of which is to determine personality by evaluating actions and reactions, behavior, movements and dreams, and thus it has succeeded in penetrating into the most deeply hidden secrets of a character.

Among the main sources of evaluation are a person's "expressive movements," i.e., his gestures, his bearing, and similar actions that can be observed visually. Small gestures accompanying the spoken word can be more revealing than entire sentences, especially when we keep in mind that the spoken word originates in conscious thought, and that it is calculated to serve a purpose. An accompanying gesture, however, is an action performed without awareness or conscious control on behalf of the speaker, and springs from the unconscious. This makes the gesture a far more illustrative source of information. There are speakers who combine softspoken messages with forceful hand movements; any audience will readily feel the contradiction between those words and the driving power behind them.

If we agree that such "expressive movements" can be the basis of a character interpretation, we are bound to realize that writing, too, is capable of being interpreted, since writing by hand is nothing less than a reduced gesture, an expressive movement on a smaller scale.

While every other gesture or manner of expression vanishes as soon as it is made, writing remains to be studied and interpreted long after it has been produced. Therein lies the great advantage of handwriting analysis. Thorough examinations can be made, comparisons are possible, material can be collected over great periods of time. Furthermore, it is one of the few methods of analysis which do not require the active co-operation of the subject, and precludes the margin of error so frequent with other systems, especially where the subject has some advance knowledge of the test methods.

It is not surprising that soon after handwriting had become common knowledge, scholars tried to analyze and compare various manners of writing in order to find the meaning of varying features in a script, and to correlate them with the writer's traits of character. The instinctive feeling that such a connection between a character and handwriting exists led to the development of graphology.

It is not the purpose of this book to go into detail concerning the history of graphology, but it can safely be said that there is a straight line of evolution beginning with the first treatise of the Italian philosopher Baldo (1622) and leading up to the most recent handbooks which draw upon contemporary studies in the psychological and psychoanalytical fields. From its infancy graphology was part of the wide sphere of psychodiagnostic test methods, and in Europe especially it has been, and is, successfully used by institutions and private persons to investigate character. Its practical uses are as manifold as they are obvious; the worthiness of applicants for trustworthy positions can be ascertained, but in addition, the discovery of special aptitudes can be effected in education and vocational training.

There is no doubt that so-called handwriting analysts at county fairs and in night clubs jeopardize the recognition of graphology as a science in its own right, but we will do well to remember that many of the modern sciences trace their origin back to occult beginnings.

It is interesting to note that in the United States the general public is still less aware of the value and possibilities of graphology than are the psychiatrists and the physicians. The latter acknowledge that many somatic and psychological disturbances are projected in handwriting, and use the graphologists' findings in their diagnosis.

Skepticism and latent suspicion will be readily overcome if we prove handwriting to be an expressive movement in its own right.

The usual objection is that we all learn to write in school, and that it is the teacher who makes us write the way we do. Nothing can be further from the truth or more superficial than such a statement. Looking at the copybooks of pupils who have passed the first steps of conscientiously copying the letter forms, we shall find that every child has already developed a handwriting of his own. The teacher will recognize the author of every script by the style of its handwriting, and without looking for the student's name. With advancing age and the development of the personality, a handwriting will show similar developments and the pattern will become more distinctive and unique with the years. Just as no two people will ever have the same fingerprints, so will no two people ever have the same handwriting. Personality and the individuality of writer and handwriting are inseparable.

It is also frequently argued that, as writing is governed by muscle contractions, it is dependent on the physical characteristics of the writer. Thousands of experiments have proved this common assumption also to be wrong. Amputees who have lost their right hand and have been forced to write lefthanded have shown, soon after they became accustomed to that change, exactly the same pattern of writing as before. From a graphological point of view the features which allow and govern analysis remained the same. Writing, therefore, is not a physical process but one which originates in the brain of the writer. The muscle contractions are, like any other movement of the human body, subject to orders given by the brain, which would justify the term "brainwriting" in preference to "handwriting."

Further evidence of these facts can be derived from experiments made under hypnosis. Just as all other expressive movements undergo a change according to the suggestion given under hypnosis, so a handwriting will change. A thrifty person under the hypnotic suggestion of being highly generous will produce in this hypnotic state a handwriting with all the characteristics of generosity. Through such tests much graphological data which up to the time of these experiments had been based on intuition or assumption, was finally verified and given its experimental foundation.

When we agree that handwriting is brainwriting, and that it is one of the expressive movements which allow deductions as to the character of the author, we still have to check the real meaning of such expressive movements.

9

Writing is consciously directed by the writer to fulfill the purpose of communicating a message. The contents are the products of a conscious process of thinking; the writing itself, however, is done quite unconsciously, at least in all such cases where the writer has fully mastered penmanship. The latter fact automatically precludes — at least for the beginner — the evaluation of handwriting of persons who are partly illiterate, and who in writing must still divide their attention between the writing process and the message. From a graphological point of view such writing is still a kind of drawing. The writing of half illiterates is nothing other than a conscious copying of letter forms, and the product of constant concentration upon their pattern. Free expressive drawing, however, like doodling, can be an excellent source of information.

A free writing, as distinguished from conscious copying, disregarding whether the writer is proficient or not, is the movement forming the basis of our examination. In fulfilling the purpose of communication such movement is directed to the addressee. As it originates in the "Ego" and is directed to the "You," the writing movement shows the path of the expression. The great Swiss graphologist Max Pulver, in his book *Symbolik der Handschrift,* was the first to reduce the entire doctrine of graphology to the words: "Writing is the path leading from the "I" to the "You"; it is the bridge over which the communication moves from the "Ego" to the "environment."

In the same manner in which a speaker discloses his unconscious thoughts by accompanying an oral message with gestures, the writer expresses his unconscious feelings by illuminating the written message with the movements of his pen. According to his character, such movements will show either a straightforward direction or a labyrinth of detours; it will make its way through higher or lower regions; it will stop or even show a tendency to return to the "Ego." In other words, by following this meandering path which leads from the "I" to the "You," we are able to discern even the most subtle traits in the personality of the writer.

In this manner of examination lies the fundamental progress of modern graphology. In the French school of graphology, at the end of the nineteenth century, single letter forms were the main source of information. In their more intuitive way of observation these early graphologists found a relationship between different patterns of letter forms and some character traits of the writer, but overlooked only too frequently the over-all picture of the script. By analyzing the expression of the writing movement in its entirety we come much closer to the basic characteristics of a personality; the danger of tracing details which often are the consequence of outside influence is greatly minimized.

Thus the tables in this book are not meant to explain single, self-dependent features of a handwriting, but should help analyze inter-connected groups of features. For this purpose systematic tables that divide the movement of writing into small subdivisions are provided. Through these it will be easier for the analyst to investigate patterns of movement, and to follow the path from the "I" to the "You" by scrutinizing it from every possible angle.

These tables are based on the experience gained from studies of all the schools of graphology. They were compiled, developed and tested through thirty-five years of practical and scientific work by the author. They will help to give a clear and concise picture of different character traits expressed through different patterns of movement.

In his first attempts the beginner will find that it is not always easy to detect the pattern of writing movement; but a thorough study of the accompanying illustrations and growing experience will help him in recognizing the important features, and permit the application of the tables.

Before going into detail about the use of the tables, it may be necessary to outline the fundamental exigencies for an analysis:

(1) At least one specimen of not less than fifteen to twenty lines is required. This should not be written for the purpose of an analysis, or at least the writer should not know of the intended analysis. There is obvious reason for this requirement, as every writer, knowing that his handwriting will be examined, immediately concentrates on the art of writing, thus not producing an unconscious movement which alone allows the tracing of a true picture of personality. It would be exactly the same as if a person, before being subjected to a Rorschach or any other test, were familiar with the exact meaning that would be attached to his answers.

There is no doubt that additional specimens give a clearer picture and will facilitate a more precise analysis. The remarks under the

11

heading "Direction of Lines" show how prevailing moods at the moment of writing can influence certain features. By using many specimens we eliminate the risk of being misled by a handwriting produced under abnormal outer influence.

The sample should be written in ink. With some experience, the beginner will soon be able to determine pressure and other features which are influenced by the writing medium, even where a pencil is employed. At first, however, ink-written specimens make the examination of the different patterns of movement easier.

(2) The age and sex of the writer should be known, as neither are part of the character image of a person. The fact that this information is needed does not constitute an admission of any shortcomings of this science.

It is clear that there are men with female traits, and women with male characteristics. In both cases such contradictory features will be expressed in the handwriting. For a precise study of character the actual sex of the writer must be of importance.

The same applies to the age of the writer. There are handwritings of young persons showing senility and similarly misleading exceptions with opposite trends.

The age of the writer is less important than the sex, but it will nevertheless add to the accuracy of the analysis if we have reasonably reliable data about the writer's age.

The Application of the Tables

At the head of the tables the reader will find two sections which need further explanation.

(1) The Different Zones of Writing and Their Meaning

We divide every handwriting into three different zones of writing:

The **"middle zone,"** which consists of all the small letters such as a, c, e, i, m, etc.

The **"upper zone"** with all letters which have an upward extension, such as b, d, h, k, l, etc., also all capitals.

12

The **"lower zone"** with all letters which extend downward such as
g, j, p, q, y, and z.

The "f" is the only small letter which occupies all three zones.

Some capitals such as G, Y, and Z also extend both up and down.

There is also a **left** and a **right** to every handwriting. When writing is the path that leads from the "I" to the "You," every detour in any zone as well as any deviation to the left or the right must have some connection with the subconscious.

The basic explanation of what is meant by **left** and **right** follows naturally when we consider that every western writing system goes from left to right. When we start writing and touch the paper with the tip of our pen, this point, at that moment, constitutes our "Ego" in the present. In proceeding, our pen moves towards the "You," into the future, in the direction of our goal, while everything written previously becomes the past, and symbolizes the part of our "Ego" which is the sum of our past experiences. The more easily and faster our pen flows to the right, the stronger is our desire to get in touch with the "You," with our goal, with the future; in short, it indicates our impulses of "extroversion." Every interruption of this right-tending movement (provided that stops are not prescribed by the standard letter form) is an indication of inner difficulties in approaching the "You." Furthermore, every stroke that according to the school pattern should tend to the right but actually goes back to the left, returns to the "Ego," and to the past, indicating even more strongly the writer's inhibitions concerning an undisturbed approach to his environment. His impulses are retractive, return to his "Ego"; in other words, show "introversion."

The three **horizontal** zones and their symbolic values are connected with the age-old association with the terms "heaven," "earth," and "hell." Heaven is above = the upper zone; earth is our daily life = the middle zone, and hell is below = the lower zone. The line on which we write, whether printed or not, is the ground on which we walk.

At a first glance these statements seem to be based on mere speculation; but the experience of graphologists over a long period of time proves their correctness. Psychoanalysis arrived at similar results by dividing the personality structure in three zones: the Superego, the Ego and the Id.

13

In accepting this doctrine, we find:

In the upper zone: the projection of the conscience; the intellectual, spiritual, religious-ethical thoughts and feelings;

In the middle zone: the projection of the daily life with its likes and dislikes; the connection with the "You" and the environment;

In the lower zone: the projection of all the unconscious motives and impulses which influence the conscious life; the urges and drives; the erotic-sexual sphere; the instinct.

There is, of course, a "left" and "right" to each of these three zones, and we often find that the movement of writing in a script shows, for example, a right-tendency in the upper zone combined with a left-tendency in one of the other two zones. Many similar combinations are possible and occur frequently.

It is therefore imperative for a good analyst to check thoroughly in which zone the outstanding features of a handwriting are located, also in which direction they move. Only by such means can the analyst link the evaluation of these features to the corresponding sphere of the writer's personality structure.

(2) Form Level

Before we start the examination of a handwriting specimen according to its single features, we must acquire a primary impression of the writing as a whole. The first impression contains the total sum of all features to be analyzed, and will disclose the form level of the script, and thereby the form level of the writer.

The ability to evaluate the writer's personality in its entirety, to see him as a whole, is the basis of a good analysis. This ability will help determine the intellectual maturity of the writer, his inner stability and independence.

Psychology knows that one trait of character may have different meanings depending on the personality, in which it is found. We know, for example—see Table II—that the size of the writing indicates the degree of the writer's self-assessment. A very sizeable script, i.e., a high degree of self-assessment, means on the positive side: self-

14

reliance, superiority, pride. On its negative side it shows: haughtiness, boastfulness, or even arrogance.

The analyst would therefore be at a loss if he should try to make deductions only according to the tables of single features. Only after having first reached an impression of the over-all personality of the writer will he know clearly which line to follow in his evaluation. The higher the standard of the form level of the handwriting, the more the evaluation of the single feature tends to the positive side. The lower, the more it tends to the negative. In a medium form level, the same character trait may have a positive as well as a negative meaning, as other traits of character evaluated out of other features in the handwriting may indicate.

The importance of such a pre-analysis cannot be overestimated. At first the beginner may have some difficulties in grading a handwriting specimen, but a strict examination, following the three components as mentioned in the section referring to form level, and especially experience, will help him arrive at the right decision.

In any case, he should not start to analyze the different features without first acquainting himself with the specimen in its entirety.

After such a preview he can use the tables successfully.

The specimens of handwritings associated with the tables will help to relate the terms used to the different features in writing. The analyst will easily detect whether a handwriting is regular or irregular, large or small, wide or narrow, etc. With such knowledge the application of the evaluating data found in the tables should not be too difficult.

Soon the graphologist will discern the interconnection of the different features, and will find that the same trait of character expresses itself in different features. He will find, for example, that a high emotionality expresses itself in the irregularity of the script, in its width, its slant, its form of connections, and more. In this way he always has the possibility of testing previous findings through later tables, and on finding contradictory features he can double-check where necessary. The analyst may frequently find a mistake in his first evaluation of a handwriting feature, but sometimes contradictory features remain. These are the cases where the complexity of human nature can be seen, graphologically, and it is here that the experience

15

and intuition of the graphologist must combine the contradictory traits into a logical and comprehensive picture.

There are two ways of making an analysis. The easier one is the enumeration of the different traits, without attempting to combine them into a picture. This, in a way, resembles the painting method of the pointillists, who by putting one color point beside the other leave it to the eye of the spectator to blend all the points into a picture.

The second and more difficult way is a comprehensive description of the writer's personality. This method presupposes a sound knowledge of psychology, and furthermore intuition, on the part of the analyst. There can be no doubt that knowledge of the graphological data alone will be insufficient to the sound analyst. Generally, however, persons interested in graphology have a good knowledge of psychology, and if not, will soon be encouraged to study the main features of this science, to further their abilities in the field of handwriting analysis.

The Different Zones of Writing and Their Meaning

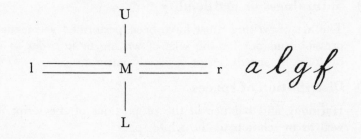

U = Upper zone = "Super-Ego" = conscience, intellectual, spiritual, ethical-religious thoughts and feelings.

M = Middle zone = "Ego" = individual consciousness as well as daily routine.

L = Lower zone = "Id" = unconscious motives of the conscious life, erotic-sexual urges and drives, materialistic impulses, instinct.

l = left = Relations to the "Self" and the past, introversion.

r = right = Relations to the "You" and the future, extroversion.

Form Level

To be evaluated out of three components of the script:

1) Naturalness or artificiality

The act of writing must have been performed as means of expression and not for the sake of writing or in order to impress by form. A speedy script is mostly natural.

2) Distribution of spaces

Harmony and balance in the proportions of the script itself as well as in relation to the white spaces.

3) Originality of letter-forms

Maturity in the creation of letters, but not eccentricity. To what degree has the writer overcome the conventional school pattern? Practical letter combinations.
Simplification without impairing legibility.

Before starting the evaluation of any feature of the script, a thorough examination of the form level must take place. This examination shows the over-all level of the writer's personality and gives an indication whether the trait of character of the different features is to be found in the positive or negative column of the following tables or in both of them.

18

Form Level

terrible accident h papers say he was

1) **Naturalness:**   Very good

2) **Distribution of spaces:**   Excellent

3) **Originality of letter forms:**   Full maturity in the execution of the letter forms. Simplifications as "t" in "terrible," "p" in "papers" and "s" in "say." These letter forms are reduced to their skeleton form without impairing their legibility. Practical letter combinations as "d-e" in "accident." Even connections between two words to increase the speed of writing as the connection "says-he."

Form level: Very good

Form Level

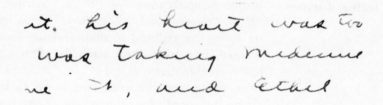

1) **Naturalness:** Good. Very speedy script

2) **Distribution of spaces:** Very good between the words as well as between the lines

3) **Originality of letter forms:** Reduced letter forms without impairing legibility except "y" in "you," which can be recognized only in its context. Good combination between the i-dot and the following letter in "quite," and the combination "d-v" in "advice."

Form level: Better than good

1) **Naturalness:** Very natural and speedy handwriting

2) **Distribution of spaces:** Good between the words as well as between the lines

3) **Originality of letter forms:** Mostly conventional letters but much maturity in their execution. Letters are simplified without impairing their legibility.

Form level: Above medium

20

Form Level

who came in with
n their last trip,
up here that he

1) **Naturalness:** Very natural handwriting without any artificiality

2) **Distribution of spaces:** Good between the words as well as between the lines

3) **Originality of letter forms:** The script is in conformity with the school pattern and shows no originality. Typical for good but conventional handwriting.

Form level: Slightly above medium

is easy to fix, tho,
Just ask any cle.

1) **Naturalness:** Good

2) **Distribution of spaces:** Good between the words but only medium between the lines

3) **Originality of letter forms:** Medium. The letter forms adhere to the conventional school pattern.

Form level: Medium

21

Form Level

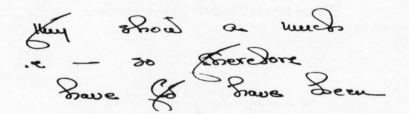

1) **Naturalness:**   Very unnatural handwriting. Writer wants to impress by form

2) **Distribution of spaces:**   Good

3) **Originality of letter forms:**   The originality in his handwriting is intentional and close to eccentricity. Writer adheres to an almost automatical pattern disregarding legibility.

Form level: Slightly below medium

1) **Naturalness:**   Very unnatural handwriting. Many artificial flourishes

2) **Distribution of spaces:**   Medium. The spaces between the words are too wide in relation to the size of the writing.

3) **Originality of letter forms:**   Many letter forms show originality. This however, does not indicate maturity but acting. The t-bars and the "b" in "been" show useless flourishes which impair the legibility.

Form level: Below medium

22

Form Level

1) **Naturalness:**   Unnatural handwriting.

2) **Distribution of spaces:**   Below medium. The spacing between the words as well as between the lines is bad. The overall picture of the script is confusing.

3) **Originality of letter forms:**   The letter forms are conventional but highly distorted.

Form level: Below medium

23

I. Regularity and Irregularity

To be evaluated out of three components of the script:

1) Degree of regularity of the height of the downstrokes in the middle zone

2) Degree of regularity in the relation between the height and the distance of the downstrokes of the middle zone

3) Degree of the regularity of the slant.

REGULARITY

Dominance of Control

positive
firmness
resistance
resolution
decisiveness
endurance
stability
orderliness
consequence
inner security
calmness
moderation
contemplation
harmony
self-conquest
self-denial
aesthetic sense

negative
coldness
constriction
indifference
stereotypy
being boring
pedant
apathy
unimpressionability
rigidity
dullness
stiffness

Regularity and Irregularity

~a while it seemed that
back or reach an
~ quite an eventual trip
terrifically; especially cause

Regular

Thursday afternoon and the
stayed here the night befo
proceeding to Los Angeles
part of the West Coast.

Regular

so it be long now u
arrives. I know yo
t be looking forwar

Regular

26

Regularity and Irregularity

IRREGULARITY

Dominance of Emotion

positive

emotionality
impulsivity
vivaciousness
creativeness
warmth
impressionability
sensitivity
openmindedness
motility
spontaneity
elasticity

negative

inconstancy
irresolution
indecision
inconsequence
irritability
excitability
fickleness
distractability
capriciousness
lack of balance
lack of direction
lack of purpose
lack of observation
curiosity
moodiness
faultfinding

Regularity and Irregularity

this didnt happen on your trip to New York otherwise we'd

Slightly irregular

about my summer plans as yet but will let you know as soon as they are definite

Irregular in height and slant

Regularity and Irregularity

basement but it hardly seemed the place to say anything. I thought you had received my letter about

Irregular in height, width, and slant

Regards to you you again,

Irregular in height, width, and slant

II. The Absolute Size of the Script

To be evaluated out of the size of the *small* letters; about 3 mm or ⅛ inch is the normal size.

A. *Fundamentally as Indicator of Self-Assessment*

LARGE SIZE

positive	*negative*
self-reliance	haughtiness
pride	pomp
noblesse	grandiosity
chivalry	boastfulness
seriousness	imperiousness
solemnity	pretentiousness
superiority	conceit
generosity	arrogance

Absolute Size

ulld complete supervision
+ do normal exercise. Thu

Large: The small letters are larger than 1/8 inch.

Such a pleasure to see
after so many years,

Medium: The small letters are about 1/8 inch.

Absolute Size

SMALL SIZE

positive	*negative*
modesty	faintheartedness
contentment	lack of self-confidence
respectfulness	self-torture
devotion	pusillanimity
tolerance	fear
peacefulness	inferiority feelings
humility	

Category of Brides who use

Small: The smaller letters are smaller than 1/8 inch.

The Absolute Size of the Script

B. *In Combination with a <u>Regular</u> Script as Indicator of Will Power*

LARGE SIZE

positive
activity
enterprise
leadership
independence
farsightedness
long term planning
talent for organization
expansion

negative
domineering
inconsiderateness
poorness of observation
project-making
vagueness of concepts
lack of concentration

Absolute Size in Combination
with a Regular Script

I just wasn't any
I admit it. Frankly

Large and very regular

The rudiments of it in some
even if you have never

Large and regular

Absolute Size in Combination
with a Regular Script

Used the regular
'it - left footing - with
'g at the start making
- Ended with Right

Large and regular

The Absolute Size of the Script

B. *In Combination with a Regular Script as Indicator of Will Power*

SMALL SIZE

positive	*negative*
concentration	pedantry
conscientiousness	pettiness
accuracy	fussiness
scrutiny of observation	despondency
control	submissiveness
	overscrupulousness

Absolute Size in Combination
with a Regular Script

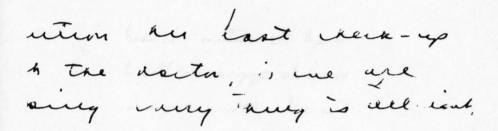

Small and regular

Small and regular

Absolute Size in Combination with a Regular Script

used the western – he used
emed to approach the l
r ine his arms a great

Small and regular

adore receiving th
us and know c
uld be a must

Small and very regular

The Absolute Size of the Script

C. *In Combination with an Irregular Script as Indicator of Emotions*

LARGE SIZE

positive	*negative*
enthusiasm	lack of sense of reality
emotional depth	distractability
idealism	exaltation
extravagance	lack of care
passionateness	partiality
fanaticism	eccentricity
	inner conflicts

Absolute Size in Combination
with an Irregular Script

Rodin's Thinker ok like a vacant-minded moron

Large and irregular

wer my coming back? Whi be drafted — Bil Conscription act ha modified that u

Large and irregular

Absolute Size in Combination
with an Irregular Script

Large and very irregular

The Absolute Size of the Script

C. *In Combination with an Irregular Script as Indicator of Emotions*

SMALL SIZE

positive	*negative*
realism	dryness
matter-of-factness	lack of enthusiasm
delicacy	prosiness
impartiality	lack of elasticity
	sterility

Absolute Size in Combination with an Irregular Script

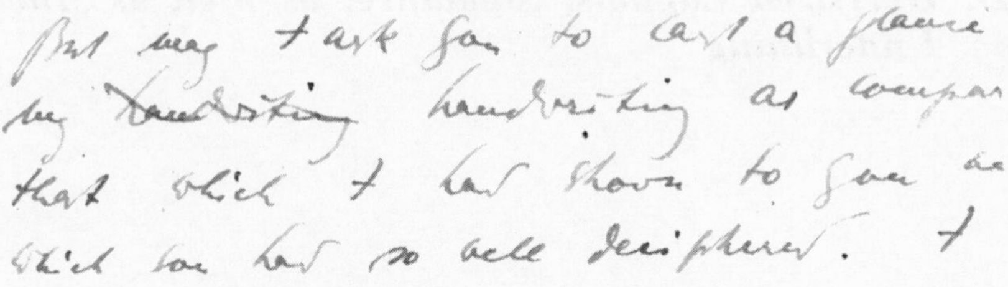
But may I ask you to cast a glance
my handwriting handwriting as compar
that which I have shown to you an
which you have so well deciphered. I

Small and irregular

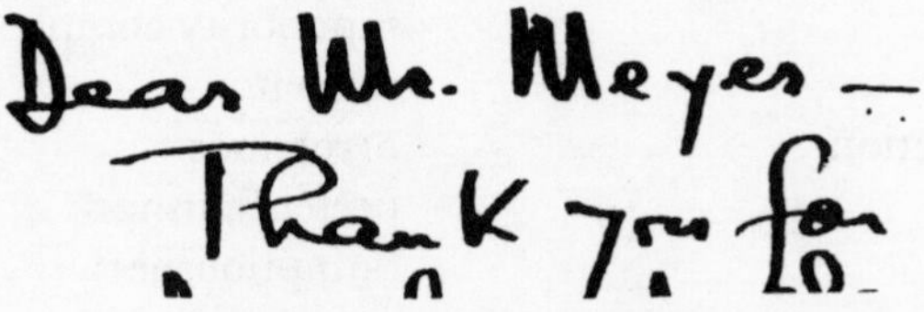
Dear Mr. Meyer—
Thank you for

Small and irregular

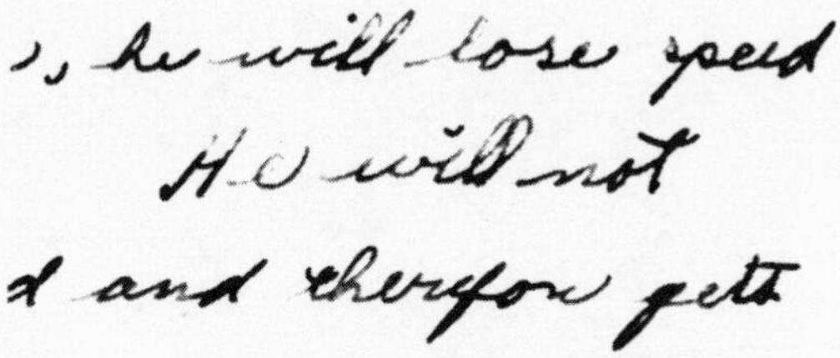
, he will lose speed
H. O will not
d and therefore gets

Small and irregular

The Absolute Size of the Script

D. *Oversized Capitals, Signature, as Well as Much Underlining*

positive	negative
desire for greatness	vanity
sense of honor	passion for glory
self-confidence	haughtiness
pride	superiority complex
leadership	conceit
sense of distinction	arrogance
	pretentiousness
	bumptiousness

Absolute Size

Next Tuesday is "Men Day - We glye flower

Oversized capitals

— "3 beg for to return & to keep secret — not to U.K., but to somewhere else, right away!/ Trinidad, trick, N days

Much underlining

III. The Relative Size of the Script

The relative size is to be seen in the relationship of the proportions of the different zones of writing.

A. *Discrepancy of Upper and Lower Zone in Relation to a Normal Middle Zone*

Oversized Upper *and* Lower Zone but *Normal* Middle Zone

positive	*negative*
ambition	discontentment
enterprise	self-accentuation
organization	discrepancy between "would" and "could"
assiduity	
farsightedness	thoughtlessness
liveliness of interests and impulses	compulsiveness
	lack of concentration
imagination	braggart
	adventurous

The Relative Size

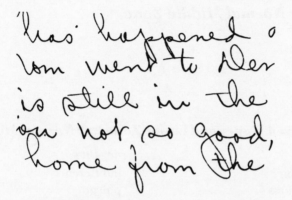

**Oversized upper and lower zones but
normal middle zone**

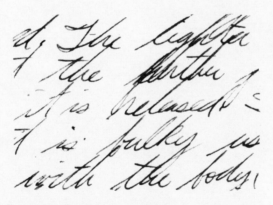

**Oversized upper and lower zones but
normal middle zone**

The Relative Size

A. *Discrepancy of Upper and Lower Zone in Relation to a Normal Middle Zone*

Undersized Upper *and* Lower Zone but *Normal* Middle Zone

positive	*negative*
observation	indifference
moderateness	phlegm
self-enjoyment	apathy
contemplativeness	indolence
contentment	dullness
modesty	
solidity	

The Relative Size

by the end of the week — if
sure I can get them either

**Undersized upper and lower zones but
normal middle zone**

if would see
if went down

**Undersized upper and lower zones but
normal middle zone**

and all the new are
made, your new
is rest of it.
nothing has changed

**Undersized upper and lower zones but
normal middle zone**

The Relative Size of the Script

B. *Oversized Middle Zone with Reduced Upper and Lower Zone*

positive	*negative*
richness of inner values	egocentricity
enthusiasm	self-love
desire for greatness	eccentricity
emotional depth	delusion of grandeur
social activities	fondness for comfort

The Relative Size

Oversized middle zone with reduced upper and lower zones

Oversized middle zone with reduced upper and lower zones

The Relative Size of the Script

C. *Discrepancy Between Upper and Lower Zone*

Predominance of upper zone

positive	*negative*
mental motility	flightiness
imagination	lack of "roots"
idealism	extravagance
abstract thinking	fickleness
intelligence	pretension
	speculation

The Relative Size

love to you
Kind wishes to you

Predominance of upper zone

the lovely lazy s
they are so handy
and we like it v
we will enjoy us

Predominance of upper zone

deshalb   Schwierigkeiten

Predominance of upper zone

53

The Relative Size

C. *Discrepancy Between Upper and Lower Zone*

Predominance of lower zone

positive

earthiness
practical inclination
realism
matter-mindedness
fondness for physical exercise

negative

heaviness
clumsiness
immobility
sensuality
anti-intellectualism
materialism
voraciousness

The Relative Size

The size and —
determine the ~
the necessity
greatest power.

Predominance of lower zone

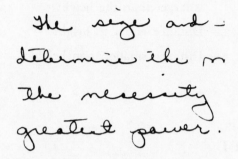

Predominance of lower zone

apology for the long
your letters — half
all my fault.
In Tues

Predominance of lower zone

IV. Width and Narrowness

Wide script = Distance between the down-strokes of small letters is larger than the height:

Normal = Distance equal to height:

Narrow = Distance smaller than height:

WIDE SCRIPT

Extroversion

positive

with pressure
elan
active ambition
drive
frankness
sociability
spontaneity
expansion

pressureless
sympathy
impressionability
vivacity
generosity
simplicity
imagination

negative

with pressure
lack of self-control
lack of reserve
lack of discipline
rashness
tactlessness
recklessness

pressureless
carelessness
impatience
prodigality
superficiality
haste
negligence

Width and Narrowness

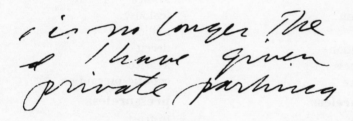

I am enclosing a few
stickers for the benefit

Wide

i is no longer the
d I have given
private parking

Wide

it shows inherent
-fully aware of. I
teresting because

Wide to normal

Width and Narrowness

NARROW SCRIPT

Introversion

positive	*negative*
with pressure	**with pressure**
self-control	coolness
slowness	criticism
reason	aridity
inhibition	jealousy
reserve	malice
moderation	deceit
tactfulness	avarice
economy	egoistic precaution
pressureless	**pressureless**
modesty	distrust
cautiousness	fear of life
contentment	neurotic inhibition
timidity	

Width and Narrowness

*The food is still good —
and by tomoro I'm pretty
about my skiing —*

Normal

*Briefe waren sehr
Arbeitest du noch
wirklich gelegentlich*

Narrow

sory, we have cancelled your

Narrow

V. Slant

In general: An *extreme* rightward (less than 55°) as well as an *extreme* leftward (over 120°) slant are to be evaluated — with few exceptions only — according to the "negative" column of the following table.

RIGHTWARD SLANT

positive	*negative*
sociability	lack of restraint
emotionability	haste
affection	restlessness
activity	lack of discipline
trust in future	excitability
devotion	thoughtlessness
impressiveness	radicalism
sympathy	distractability
adaptability	immoderateness
dexterity	verbosity
passion	hysteria
expressiveness	
initiative	

Rightward Slant

the long weekend,

how you manage

Extreme rightward slant (40° - 50°)

tion easily discouraged

', and my boys could really

Extreme rightward slant (55°)

course there wou

many different n

of substituting an

Extreme rightward slant (55°)

Rightward Slant

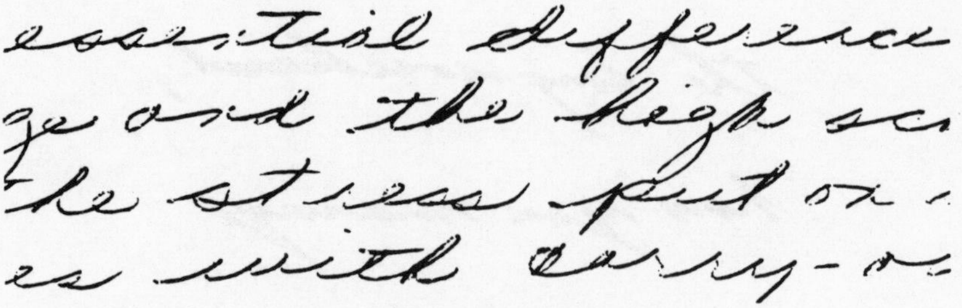

Rightward slant (65°)

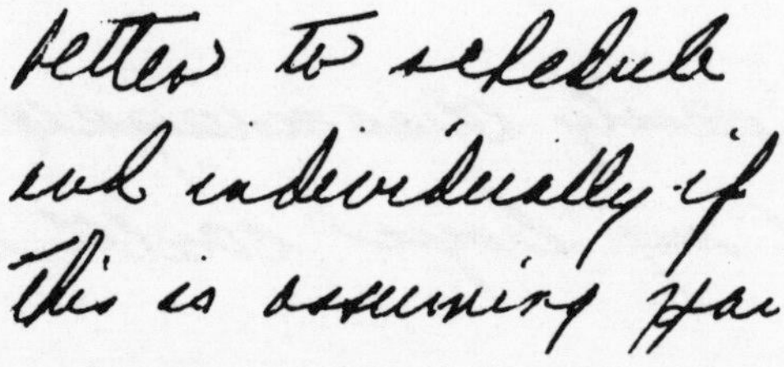

Rightward slant (75°)

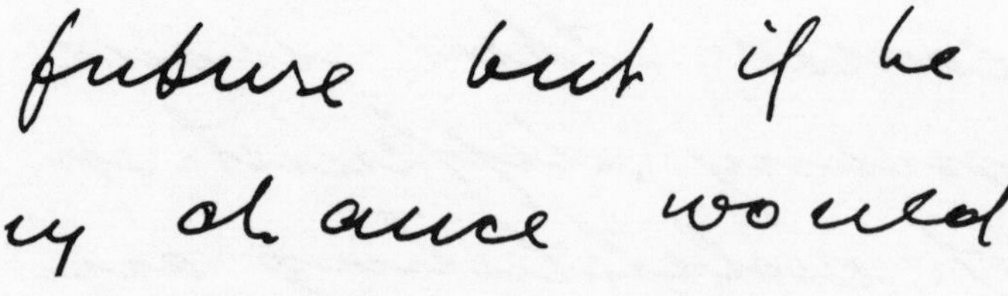

Rightward slant (75°)

Slant

VERTICAL SLANT

positive	*negative*
dominance of reason	coldness
control	lack of interest
prudence	lack of emotion
self-command	indifference
reserve	self-centredness
self-consistency	egotism
rationalism	rigidity
caution	pitilessness
skepticism	
pride	
concentration	
neutrality	
poise	

Vertical Slant

little background lead
sitting in judgment a

Vertical slant (85°)

its of endurance.
development of jud
development of men
be able to adjust to

Vertical slant (85°)

I loved yesterday

Vertical slant (85°)

Vertical Slant

*hand the mask
non, which was usually
on short only —*

Vertical slant (90°)

*Oh well, I know that
you're going to be very surprised
when you receive this letter. Tell
you the truth — I didn't expect*

Vertical slant (90°)

65

Slant

LEFTWARD SLANT

positive	*negative*
control	artificiality
reserve	affectation
self-denial	forced behavior
self-conquest	pretentiousness
precaution	conflict with reality
tradition-bound	withdrawal
fear of future	egotism
	arrogance
	conceit

Leftward Slant

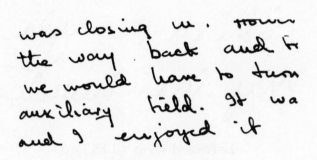

Leftward slant (100°)

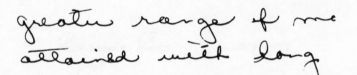

Leftward slant (100°)

Leftward slant (110°)

Leftward Slant

Leftward slant (115°)

Leftward slant (115°)

Extreme leftward slant (130°)

VI. Form of Connections

A. *Garland*

ииии

DOMINANCE OF NATURALNESS

positive	*negative*
kindness	irresolution
benevolence	indetermination
sociability	easy to influence
affirmation	weakness
tolerance	distractability
gentleness	dependency
sympathy	instability
confidence	fickleness
frankness	laziness
sincerity	curiosity
easy contact	**with wide script**
adaptability	cycloid type
hospitality	

Form of Connections. Garland

' you need many write me; I am
it much effort.

Garland

There should be no
no beginning type act
practically speaking

Garland

census taker called on
Sat, afternoon & Bobs
was the fifth one &

Garland

Form of Connections. Garland

loss occurred, the total loss being m. The question was whether cost or ? loss deduction, cost being the lower, was the basis of the loss.

Garland

Glad to see the today — tired

Garland with wide script

since you has to minds or hearts:

Garland with wide script

Form of Connections

B. *Arcade*

DOMINANCE OF RESERVE

positive	*negative*
reserve	lack of frankness
secretiveness	insincerity
formalism	artificiality
cautiousness	mannerism
distinction	affectation
sense of tradition	pretension
noblesse	distrust
taciturnity	mendacity
sense of distance	suspiciousness
skepticism	tendency to scheme

Form of Connections. Arcade

Arcade

Arcade

Form of Connections. Arcade

do your ever 7
We still have
time your work
your are welcor

Arcade

Arcade

zusammen. Ich kann Dir
'as denn Du verdammst
ausschütten. Denn Du

Arcade

Form of Connections

C. *Angles*

DOMINANCE OF STABILITY

positive
firmness
resistance
resoluteness
constancy
determination
reliability
persistence
energy
sincerity
strictness

negative
hardness
coldness
lack of sympathy
stubbornness
inadaptability
rigidity
restraint

with pressure
quarrelsomeness
aggressiveness
brutal opposition

with narrow script
schizoid type

Form of Connections. Angles

*A lot of rain here .
home is warm and
Remember to see
come three, — the li
is always out. Best*

Angles

*onderful flight and our
City arrived undamaged.
", I can recommand*

Angles

76

Form of Connections.   Angles

Angles

Angles with narrow script

Form of Connections

D. *Threads*

DOMINANCE OF LABILITY

positive	*negative*
versatility	elusiveness
flexibility	ambiguity
adaptability	insincerity
diplomacy	tactician
elasticity	mimicry
psychological talent	cunning
intelligence	lack of conscience
dexterity	nervousness
	hysteria

Form of Connections. Threads

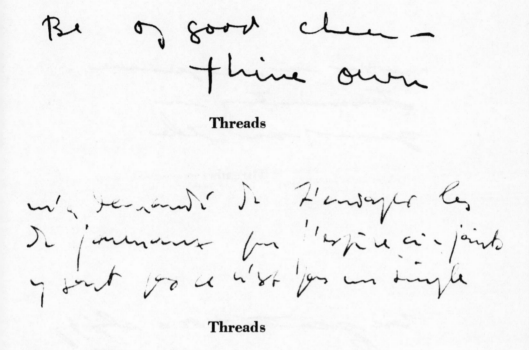

Threads

Threads

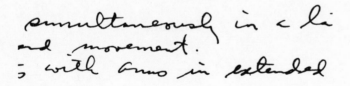

Threads

Form of Connections. Threads

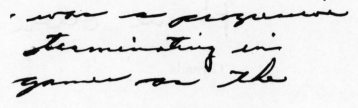

Threads

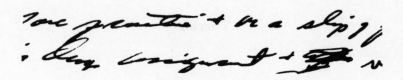

Threads

VII. Degree of Connectedness

Connected   = At least 5 letters are written in one stroke. Interruptions for the application of "i"-dots or "t"-bars do not count as such.

Disconnected = Less than 4 letters are written in 1 stroke. Type script is not a disconnected script.

Connected script

DOMINANCE OF ADAPTABILITY

positive	*negative*
consequential thinking	hastiness in drawing conclusions
planning	superificiality
premeditation	flighty thinking
logic	overadaptability
reproductive intelligence	dependency on others
cooperativeness	poverty of ideas
steadiness of work	adherence to old concepts
sociability	lack of initiative
purposefulness	

Degree of Connectedness. Connected Script

I could have shared
some of it. If you come
here I promise you

Highly connected script

Coming this way for a visit?
Time rolls on and holiday

Connected script

Degree of Connectedness. Connected Script

That was certainly a most pleasant when your announcement about marriage arrived. I wish you all

Connected script

We are having The Decoration day Holidays now and New

Connected script

The truth Being the leaving ... I could ... ing could I enjoying

Connected script

Degree of Connectedness

Disconnected script

DOMINANCE OF LACK OF ADAPTABILITY

positive	*negative*
intuitive thinking	inconsequence in thinking
independence of judgment	inconsistency
productive observation	unsociability
intellectual initiative	mental jumpiness
individualism	lack of forethought
wealth of ideas	utopism
wit	egocentricity
inventiveness	stubbornness
self-reliance	**wide, irregular**
independence	**interruptions**
	fearfulness
	loneliness
	hermit
	decay of letters
	weak-minded
	imbecile
	mental disease

Degree of Connectedness.
Disconnected Script

you this year —
— o yet so
as newer to meet.

Disconnected script

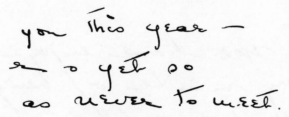

Je t'assure que rien
et on profite bien à
est usté en France. in

Disconnected script

& the weight is 4.
base of support, ea
1, and less effort

Disconnected script

Any intelligently planned
have its climax as a co
meet, demonstration, tests (

Disconnected script

Degree of Connectedness.
Disconnected Script

Disconnected script

Disconnected script with wide irregular interruptions

Disconnected script with decay of letters

VIII. Distribution of Spaces Between Words and Lines

Organization of the mind

Wide spacing

positive
orderliness of thinking
analytical thinking
clear representation of facts
cleanness
formality
musical sense
generosity
creative ability

negative
lack of spontaneity
too wide spaces with great script
lavishness
inconsiderateness
incoherence
spoiled nature
isolation (with great as well
   as with small script)

Distribution of Spaces. Wide Spacing

(handwriting sample)

**Excellent wide spacing between words as well as
between lines**

(handwriting sample)

Wide spacing between words and lines

Distribution of Spaces. Wide Spacing

Dont get to lonely, thinking of you

Wide spacing

ertainly know what can when you say am such a short

Wide spacing

hen are you coming is us? We would to see you and

Wide spacing

Distribution of Spaces. Wide Spacing

[handwriting sample]

Too wide spaces with great script

[handwriting sample]

Too wide spaces between words, normal between lines

[handwriting sample]

Too wide spaces between lines, normal between words

Distribution of Spaces Between Words and Lines

Organization of the mind

Narrow spacing

positive
instinctual thinking
spontaneity
economy

negative
pettiness
thriftiness
**uneven with entanglement
between lines**
instability
chattiness
muddled thinking
strong impulsivity
mental disturbance

Distribution of Spaces. Narrow Spacing

Narrow spacing (in proportion to the size of the script)

Narrow spacing

Narrow spacing

Distribution of Spaces. Narrow Spacing

Narrow spacing (in proportion to the size of the script)

**Uneven narrow spacing with entanglement between
the lines**

IX. Direction of Lines

If one has only one specimen of a handwriting at hand for an analysis, and this specimen shows either ascending lines (B) or descending lines (C) and there are no other features in this specimen which support the above mentioned traits of character, it is safer to omit the evaluation of the directions of lines. In such a case this specimen may have been written in a mood which has nothing to do with the normal mood of the writer. These two directions of lines are too much depending on the mood of the moment so that only a repetition in several specimens allows the statement that the indicated mood is prevailing in the writer.

A. *Horizontal Straight*

positive	negative
steadfastness	dullness
perseverance	lack of vivacity
orderliness	lack of emotions
methodicalness	

Direction of Lines. Horizontal Straight

Appreciate — but he seemes
to be rid of it. — As to the
old acquaintance, his life
Thanks for your interest.

with beaches which are
just like the French &
When you come East

was under the impression
I had more, but this
seems to be it. I have
been asking around

the way home he took us
+ tree's in blossom it was
. the road along the Valley

Direction of Lines

B. *Ascending Straight*

positive
zeal
ambition
pushing spirit
elation
devotion to a purpose
singlemindedness
communicativeness
optimism

negative
excitability
restlessness
loquacity
frivolity
anger

in terms of daily
instead of the deep
brought out. Whi
to find my habit
there might be n
criticism than you
. I than

Hello!
Sorry we haven't
have been so bu
our house (the on
. . . , . I leave our ;

was down mou .
on my two feet. The s.
sides between the falls
that there

Direction of Lines

C. *Descending Straight*

positive
oversensitiveness
fatigue
depression
pessimism

negative
lack of will power
with tremor signs
illness

[handwritten sample, first specimen:]

...something to send the cheque.
...it destroyed so you can balance
your accounts! ...thanks again
Perhaps something will come

[handwritten sample, second specimen:]

overjoyed to receive your
...tter and to learn that you
...ll, and happy in your new
...nious, peaceful country.
...been so often in...

Direction of Lines. Descending Straight

ances of getting town the center lane off of the other lanes, close them and outside of the court to slow force the team to pass thus

d'un grand salon — luxurious
laurraient y tenir)
2 chambres à coucher

Direction of Lines

D. *Ascending or Descending Steps*

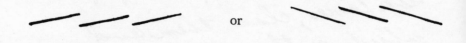 or

Indication of self-control. Writer fights against the tendencies that are outlined under B and C, being afraid to become overpowered by them.

Direction of Lines.
Ascending or Descending Steps

build a foundation in fundamentals
provide carry over activities
inspire body control
help development of whole personality

Ascending steps

Thank you very :
for your sailing letter

Ascending steps

want and he
will you know
anything Darling
pleas

Descending steps

103

Direction of Lines

E. *Wavering Lines*

positive
sensitiveness
diplomacy

negative
emotional instability
aimlessness
unsteadiness
unreliability

that you will find you as I would be to join a class

the I owe you an
delay in answering

you, I hope this
reaches you, you
did not put on an

I say again, I am
for hurting you in any
last thing on earth
want to do to you.

Direction of Lines

F. *Convex Lines*

Flaring zeal and ambition but without perseverance

G. *Concave Lines*

Initial self-distrust which slowly gains courage to act

*would never take us ~ -
destination. He ear was about
~ 1939 Plymouth, which sounds
~ ~ . Model t*

Convex lines

Direction of Lines. Convex and Concave Lines

Will I have to say good-bye
now and take my shower but I

Convex lines

with a terrible cold, who was it
and I was the nurse. However h
he is frustrated and aspirined
to perfect health and I am in

Concave lines

Catherine a grossi un peu mais, comme
le ça ne se voit pas beaucoup, parce qu

Concave lines

Direction of Lines

H. *Straight Lines but Overcrowded at the End and Going Up- or Downward*

_____/   or   ⎯⎯⎯⎯⎯⎯⎯⎯

Writer overshoots his aim on account of lack of economy or thought-lessness. Rhetoric eloquence of an enthusiast who overestimates his own opinion.

Straight lines but overcrowded at the end

X. Margins

A. *Upper Margin*

wide	*narrow*
respectfulness	informality
formality	obtrusiveness

B. *Lower Margin* (not very important)

wide	*narrow*
aesthetic sense	communicativeness
reserve	

C. *Left Margin* (often omitted in American scripts)

wide	*narrow*
generosity	thriftiness
lavishness	lack of form sense
pride	informality

widening	*narrowing*
obliviousness	initial formality
unsuccessful desire to overcome the natural tendency to lavishness	unsuccessful desire to overcome the natural tendency to thriftiness
	precaution

Margins

D. *Right Margin*

wide
fear of future
precaution
reserve

widening
growing suspicion

narrow
communicativeness
vitality
haste

narrowing
initial shyness

E. *Four Exact Margins*

positive
aesthetic form sense
reserve
pride

negative
stylishness
overformality
vanity
isolation

F. *All Four Margins Missing*

positive
wide interests
hospitality
kindness

negative
lack of reserve
lack of taste
curiosity

XI. Speed of Writing

Indications of speed: Fluent unbroken strokes; ascending lines; "i"-dots and "t"-bars are placed to the right of the stem; letters at the end of words become incomplete; no unnecessary adjustments; high degree of connectedness; width of the script; rightward slant; rounded connections, and dominance of right-tending movements

Indications of slowness: Artificiality of the script; descending lines; "i"-dots and "t"-bars straight over or to the left of the stem; increase of size at the end of words; ornamentation; narrow script; leftward slant; angular connections, and dominance of left-tending movements

A. *Quick Writing*

positive	*negative*
naturalness of expression	hastiness
self-assurance	flightiness
initiative	rashness
agility	superficiality
purposefulness	instability
impulsiveness	irritability
spontaneity	planlessness
impatience	unsteadiness
vivacity	unreliability
generosity	
extroversion	

Speed of Writing. Quick Writing

here is about 10 ∴ more than ~~at~~ you market.

wouldn't 'bother to up, maybe will he d surely before we go

:signs for furniture and colour schemes and verings, design of the , for the projection box,

the em-
screeches. Anyway,
a long story short,
finally started out.

together at that level —
that he disappearing
all the way through.

Speed of Writing. Medium Speed

the toward the more
will be gotten n.
There must be a .
between the two
one cannot fine
the other.

should be more than cov
should be helped to reali

Speed of Writing. Medium Speed

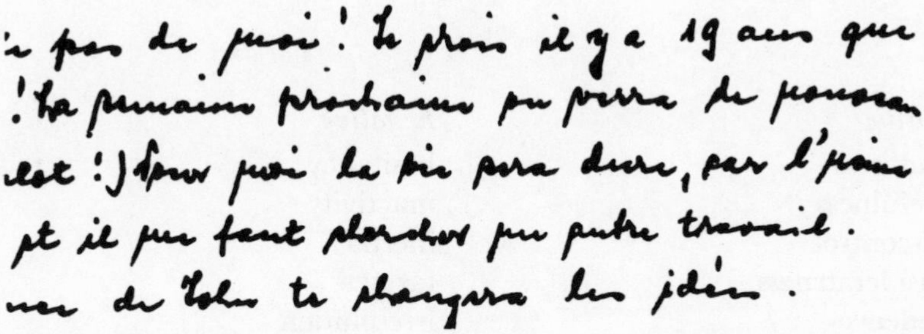

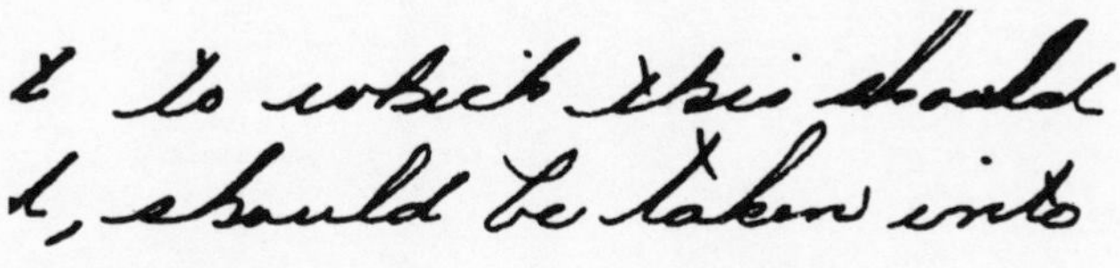

[handwritten text in French, partially legible]

*... pas de quoi! Je crois il y a 19 ans que
! ta semaine prochaine ... pourra de ...
...) pour moi la vie sera dure, par l'...
... il ... faut ... par ... travail.
... de ... te changera les idées .*

*to which this should
, should be taken into*

Speed of Writing

B. *Slow Writing*

positive	*negative*
steadiness	hesitancy
carefulness	inactivity
self-control	inertia
considerateness	laziness
prudence	irresolution
caution	slow thinking
coolheadedness	weak will
economy	indolence
introversion	dullness
	insincerity

Speed of Writing. Slow Writing

days and other items connec
I think the material is very
lly so since it is written esp

Have a inventory at the beginning
supplies and etc. and have one of

HCK. - The country up here is most
scenic and the children may run to
their hearts desire. We think of you

117

*I am happy.
in California I've.
the weather is "u
at times.*

*To-day is May Day!
are we thrilled?*

XII. Left- and Right-tending Movements

Indications of left-tending movement: Strokes which according to the school pattern should be written with a right-tending movement are either omitted or written with a left-tending movement.

Examples:

in upper zone: *[handwriting samples]*   instead of *[handwriting samples]*

in middle zone: *[handwriting samples]* instead of *[handwriting samples]*

in lower zone: *[handwriting samples]*   instead of *[handwriting samples]*

Indications of right-tending movement: Strokes which according to the school pattern should be written with a left-tending movement are either omitted or written with a right-tending movement.

Examples:

in upper zone: *[handwriting samples]*   instead of *[handwriting samples]*

in middle zone: *[handwriting samples]*

     instead of *[handwriting samples]*

in lower zone: *[handwriting samples]*   instead of *[handwriting samples]*

119

Left- and Right-tending Movements

As a manuscript can have different tendencies of movement in the three different zones an exact examination is necessary.

The fundamental meaning of an **increase** in one of the two movements is:

Left-Tending Movement

passiveness   self-knowledge
meditation   isolation
inner life   introversion

Right-Tending Movement

action   tendency to leadership
activity   progression
outer life   extroversion

The meaning in detail according to the zones:

120

Left-tending Movements

Left-Tending Movement IN UPPER ZONE

positive

personal recollection
reflexiveness
meditativeness
lyrical inclination
intellectual self-dependence

negative

speculating sense
intellectual self-centredness
resentment
egocentricity

Phs

Loop on head of "P" tends to the left.
Omission of prescribed right-tending loop on head of "h"

Left-tending Movements. Upper Zone

T-bar starting with a strong left-tending movement

T-bar starting with a strong left-tending movement

Oversized left-tending loop on "G," t-bar to the left of
stem
(In lower zone:) Left-tending hook on "G"

**Upstroke on "f" too far to the left, t-bar to the left of
stem**

**"d" ends with left-tending stroke.
(In middle zone:) Left-tending small loops in "a" and
"m"**

Left-tending Movements. Upper Zone

Dauup aew

"d's" end with strong left-tending strokes.
(In middle zone:) Left-tending small loops in "m" and
   "n"

field ,

"d" ends with left-tending stroke.
(In middle zone:) Lower f-loop ends in middle zone with
   a strong left-tending movement.

Backgrounds

Upper loops left-tending
(In middle zone:) Reclined script, small left-tending
   hooks on "k" and "d"
(In lower zone:) Left-tending loop on "g"

Left-tending Movements

Left-Tending Movement IN MIDDLE ZONE

positive	*negative*
independence	egotism
self-preservation	insincerity
self-reliance	falsehood
	deceit

Sunday May 14

Oversized left-tending loop on base of "S"
Double-loops on "d" and "a"

124

Left-tending Movements. Middle Zone

T-base tending too far to the left
Double-loop on "g"
(In upper zone:) Rolled-in upstroke on "T"
　　　Omission of prescribed right-tending loop on "h"

Exaggerated left-tending loop on "S"

Reclined script
Missing upstrokes on small letters
Small left-tending hooks on "b," "l"
(In upper zone:) Upper loops bend to the left.

Omission of right-tending end-strokes on "d" and "t"

Left-tending Movements. Middle Zone

Gaeeeely

Small loops on head of "m" and "i"
(In lower zone:) Exaggerated left-tending loops of "F"
and "y"

Spend

Inverted left-tending loop on base of "S"
(In upper zone:) Prescribed right-tending loop on head
of "S" is omitted

forced

Lower loop on "f" tends straight to the left.
Omission of the right-tending small loops on "o" and "e"
(In upper zone:) Omission of right-tending loop on "f"
forming a loop

start

Left-tending loop on base of "s" (Catpaw)
Prescribed upstroke on final "t" omitted

Left-tending Movements

Left-Tending Movement IN LOWER ZONE

positive

motherly disposition
mystic impressionability
instinctive apperception of the
  past

negative

self-love
narcissism $=$ inversion of the
  libido
with pressure in lower zone
hypersensitivity in the erotic
  sphere

Lower loop on "p" extends too far to the left

Left-tending Movements. Lower Zone

My

Omission of right-tending final upstroke on "y"

wedding
... i. A Y..

Omission of right-tending final upstroke on "g"
**(In upper zone:) Downstrokes on "d" form left-tending
small loops**
**(In middle zone:) Omission of right-tending upstroke
on "w"**
Omission of the small right-tending loop on "e"

Laguna Beach,
California

Exaggerated left-tending loop on "g"
Small final hooks on "h" and "a"
(In middle zone:) Double loops in both "a" of "Laguna"

128

Left-tending Movements. Lower Zone

Rolled-in left-tending loop on "f"

Left-tending hook instead of a loop in "f"
(In middle zone:) Exaggerated left-tending stroke on base
    of "J"
Missing right-tending upstrokes on "h" and "b"
Missing right-tending end strokes on "e" and "l"
Double loops on "a"
Downstrokes on "u" forming small left-tending loops

Right-tending Movements

Right-Tending Movement IN UPPER ZONE

positive

increased intellectual approach
    to the environment
empathy

negative

suggestibility
mental hastiness
forgetfulness
rash judgment

Part

Part

Upper loop on "P" only to the right
(In middle zone:) Missing left-tending stroke on base
of "P"

130

Right-tending Movements. Upper Zone

David

Exaggerated right-tending loop on "D"
Final stroke of "d" far to the right

Tower

T-bar shows strong right-tendency
(In middle zone:) Left-tending movements stronger!!
"o" close with left-tendency
Missing right-tending upstroke on "w"
The right-tending small loop on "e" is reduced.

three

Exaggerated right-tending t-bar

Right-tending Movements. Upper Zone

"d" ending with right-tending hook
(In middle zone:) Contradictory movements:
         Left-tending: Lower loop on "d"
                 Reduced small loops
                    on "e"
                 Reclined script
       Right-tending: Loop on "p"
                 Final stroke on "p"

Exaggerated final strokes on "d's"
(In middle zone:) Wide script

T-bars to the right of stem and connected by right-tending
    strokes
(In middle zone:) The reclined script of this specimen
                 does not indicate a left-tending
                 movement
                 The tendency is stronger to the right,
                 shown especially at the base of "s"
                 where the prescribed left-tending
                 movement is omitted.

Right-tending Movements

Right-Tending Movement IN MIDDLE ZONE

positive

enterprise
sympathy
increased desire to join
unselfishness
altruism
helpfulness

negative

restlessness
unrestrained communicativeness
dependency
weakness
wastefulness
undiscriminating sociability

Please — come — any time

Even the words are connected by right-tending strokes

Right-tending Movements. Middle Zone

porn

"o" open on top by omitting the left-tending movement
that is necessary to close them

program

"o" open on top. Extended right-tending loop on "p"
Wide script
(In lower zone:) Omission of left-tending loop of "g"

committee

Wide script with threadlike connections

Right-tending Movements. Middle Zone

South   Blorles

Direct connections of "S" and "B" to the following letters

would

Prolonged final stroke of "d" drawn in the middle zone

Right-tending Movements

Right-Tending Movement IN LOWER ZONE

positive

increase in concentration
abstraction
instinctive understanding
dexterity

negative

**exaggerated length of the
right-tending final strokes:**
refusal to come in too close contact

may.

Omission of the left-tending loop on "y"

136

Right-tending Movements. Lower Zone

every thing fo

Omission of the left-tending loops on "y" and "g"
(In upper zone:) The t-bar to the left of stem indicates
    left-tendency

College

"g" is directly connected to the next letter on its right.

you

'"y" is directly connected to the next letter on its right.
(In middle zone:) "y" goes straight to the right by omit-
    ing the first downstroke.
The loop of "o" is almost a circle showing stronger ten-
    dency to the right.

Right-tending Movements. Lower Zone

questions

"q" is directly connected to the next letter to the right.
(In upper zone:) Right-tendency of t-bar, i-dot far to the
right of stem

agree

"g" is directly connected to the next letter to the right.
(In middle zone:) "g" open on top

of good

f-loop straight to the right, omitting the left-tending closing
small loop
(In middle zone:) "o," "g" and "d" loop open on top

138

Left- and Right-tending Movements in Accessory Parts

Left-Tending Movement IN ACCESSORY PARTS

Initial upstrokes with a *small* hook:

cheerfulness, joy

Rolled-in strokes at the beginning or at the end:

amiability with calculation
insincerity with politeness

The claw-stroke:

avarice

The catpaw:

falseness

The catching hook upward:

possessiveness
intellectual self-defense

Left-tending Movements in Accessory Parts

The catching hook downward:

egotism
self-preservation

Left-tending final arcade:

secretiveness
inhibition
insincerity

i-dots and t-bars to the left of the stem:

to be evaluated like the
left-tending movement
in the upper zone.

Left-tending Movements in Accessory Parts

noon

him

me

Initial upstrokes with a *small* hook

Dame

Budget

Rolled-in strokes at the beginning or the end of letters

Left-tending Movements in Accessory Parts

Rolled-in strokes at the beginning or the end of letters

Claw strokes at the end of letters or t-bars

Left-tending Movements in Accessory Parts

**The catpaw in the middle zone
as well as in the lower zone**

The catching hook upward

Left-tending Movements in Accessory Parts

better

The catching hook upward

which may result

Harding

ahn

The catching hook downward

144

Left-tending Movements in Accessory Parts

Left-tending final arcade

t-bars and i-dots to the left of stem

Right-tending Movements in Accessory Parts

Right-Tending Movement IN ACCESSORY PARTS

i-dots and t-bars to the right of the stem:

to be evaluated like
the right-tending movement
in upper zone.

exaggerated right-tending cross-bars

expansion of the "Ego"
but more in the sense of
authority than devotion

Right-tending Movements in Accessory Parts

die winter.

in .

**t-bars and i-dots to the right
of stem**

The day

**Exaggerated right-tending
cross bar**

XIII. Pressure

A. *In Combination with a Regular Script as Indicator of Will Power*

HIGH PRESSURE

positive	*negative*
energy	heaviness
endurance	clumsiness
steadiness	obstinacy
determination	stubbornness
self-control	vanity
tenacity	lack of differentiation
conscientiousness	
reliability	
fearlessness	
masculinity	

Pressure in Combination
with a Regular Script

*It was the first time
have ever been in d
desert, believe me,*

High pressure

*h a wall of human
y choice resigns her-
fluttering eyelashes*

High pressure

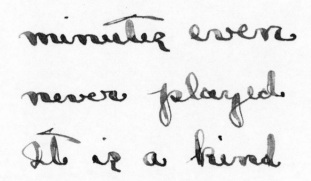

High pressure

Pressure in Combination
with a Regular Script

LOW PRESSURE

positive	*negative*
agility	lack of energy
elasticity	lack of resistance
adaptability	unsteadiness
mobility	lack of determination
modesty	lack of initiative
femininity	yieldingness

Pressure in Combination
with a Regular Script

It's a good thing comes around and oud would lose tro entirely,

Low pressure

had a severe ..e in the last onths. My doctor, ..id it was very ..nd. I'll probably

Low pressure

Pressure

B. *In Combination with an Irregular Script as Indicator of Emotions*

HIGH PRESSURE

positive
impulsiveness
vitality
resoluteness
receptivity
adaptability

negative
irritability
obstinacy
aggressiveness
excitability

With blotted pressure:
violence
brutality

Pressure in Combination
with an Irregular Script

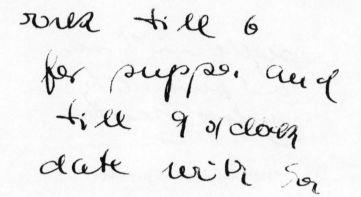

High Pressure

High Pressure

Pressure in Combination
with an Irregular Script

High and blotted pressure

Pressure in Combination with an Irregular Script

LOW PRESSURE

positive
delicacy of feeling
sensitivity
impressionability
idealism
dreaminess

negative
lability
superficiality
timidity
distraction
loftiness
weakness

Pressure in Combination
with an Irregular Script

[handwriting sample]

Low pressure

[handwriting sample]

Low pressure

XIV. Pastiness and Sharpness

Pasty Script = Upstrokes have the same thickness as downstrokes and not less than 1/50 inch.

Sharp script = Marked difference in the thickness of up- and downstrokes.

PASTY SCRIPT

positive

contemplative sensuality
warmth
color sensee
enjoying life
gourmand
impressionability
naturalness

negative

lack of spirituality
roughness
rudeness
materialistic impulses

Lower loops ink-filled:

strong sexual urges
oversexed person

Pastiness and Sharpness

Pastiness

your graphologist
when you next see

corrective and restrictive in
too much in others.
inistrative guidance and help.

here a boy who can sea
and come from behind
in many cases given

Pasty script

Pastiness and Sharpness

Pastiness

Pasty script with lower zone loops ink-filled

Pasty script with middle zone loops ink-filled

Pastiness and Sharpness

SHARP SCRIPT

positive	*negative*
spirituality	lack of sensuality
analytical mind	asceticism
self-discipline	coldness
vitality	resentment
determination	lack of apperception
pleasure in discussion	criticism
tenacity	quarrelsomeness
	hardhearted egotism
	malice

Pastiness and Sharpness

Sharpness

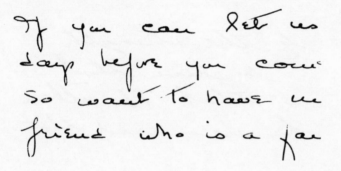

Sharp script

Pastiness and Sharpness

Sharpness

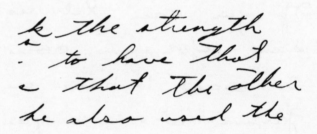

Sharp script

XV. The Execution of the Letter Forms

A. *Fullness and Leanness of the Letters*

Fullness = The letter forms enclose a larger area than prescribed by the school pattern—mainly in the looped letters.

Leanness = The letter forms enclose a smaller area than prescribed by the school pattern—mainly in the looped letters.

FULLNESS IN UPPER ZONE

positive	*negative*
imagination	fantastic boastfulness
good apperception	utopianism
mental vision	lack of self-criticism
figurative description in speech	day dreaming

The Execution of the Letter Forms.
Fullness

[signature]

Fullness in upper zone

[signature]

Fullness in upper zone

[signature]

Fullness in upper and in middle zone

The Execution of the Letter Forms. Fullness

FULLNESS IN MIDDLE ZONE

positive

warmth
heartiness
emotionality

negative

conventional amiability

Fullness in upper and in middle zone

The Execution of the Letter Forms. Fullness

[handwritten sample]

Fullness in middle zone

[handwritten sample]

Fullness in middle zone

166

The Execution of the Letter Forms. Fullness

FULLNESS IN LOWER ZONE

positive   *negative*

sensuousness   sensuality
                                              erotic fantasy

Fullness in lower zone

167

The Execution of the Letter Forms.
Fullness

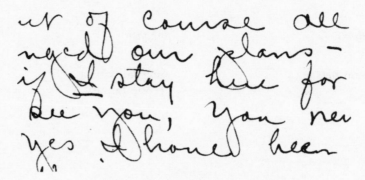

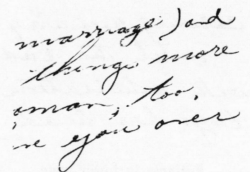

Fullness in lower zone

The Execution of the Letter Forms

Fullness and Leanness of the Letters

LEANNESS

positive   *negative*

IN UPPER ZONE

rational thinking	lack of imagination
clearsightedness	poverty of ideas
critical sense	dryness
ethical tendencies	lack of form sense
	irritability

IN MIDDLE ZONE

coolness	rigidity
matter-of-factness	poverty of inner resources

IN LOWER ZONE

realism	materialism
businessmindedness	money complex

The Execution of the Letter Forms.
Leanness

e to carry on most of the
to it the same time.

Leanness in all three zones

me or cook it when
It's a most extraor
living – going to work
Jour., listening to TL

Leanness in the upper and in the lower zone

In some sports you cannot
e your full speed all the time.
f you are a large person or

Leanness in all three zones

The Execution of the Letter Forms.
Leanness

Leanness in all three zones

Leanness in the upper and in the lower zone

Leanness in the upper and in the lower zone

Fullness in the middle zone

171

The Execution of the Letter Forms

B. *Ornamentation and Simplification*

Ornamentation = The script is ornamented by additions or flourishes which are not prescribed by the school pattern.

Simplification = The letter forms are reduced to their basic form but *without impairing the legibility* of the script. (Not to be mistaken for leanness.)

ORNAMENTATION

positive	*negative*
form sense	bad taste
pride	vanity
formality	circumstantiality
cultivation of details	vain exaggeration
creativeness	insincerity
diligence	eccentricity
originality	affectation

The Execution of the Letter Forms.
Ornamentation and Simplification

Ornamentation

The Execution of the Letter Forms.
Ornamentation and Simplification

Ornamentation

The Execution of the Letter Forms

Ornamentation and Simplification

SIMPLIFICATION

positive
sense for the essential
simplicity
matter-of-factness
clear judgment
maturity
orderliness
aesthetic sense

negative
lack of form sense
neglect
**if illegible, especially
in slow handwritings**
tactlessness
insincerity
unreliability
sloppiness

Simplification

175

The Execution of the Letter Forms
Ornamentation and Simplification

My dear Margaret.

the most beautiful
ation spots in America,

How delightful is your
she is beautiful intell
thoroughly nice —

Simplification

176

The Execution of the Letter Forms.
Ornamentation and Simplification

*Et il y a
in C lur !*

Simplification

tomorrow

Simplification, almost illegible

Pcmuc

Simplification, illegible

XVI. Address on Envelopes

Written in upper right quarter

strong but uncontrolled activity
love of independence
obtrusiveness

Written in upper left quarter

lack of confidence in future
strong influence of the past
difficulty in social contact

Written in lower right quarter

materialistic and instinctive con-
    tact to the environment
physical activity
denial of the past

Written in lower left quarter

materialistic or instinctive inhi-
    bitions
caution and suspicion

XVII. Signature

NB. A signature alone should never be the source of a reliable analysis. Its graphological value is to be found in comparison to the writer's usual handwriting in the context of the script.

Smaller than other script

writer is more modest than he demonstrates

Larger than other script

writer has more self-reliance in his private sphere than he demonstrates

Similar to other script

even nature of writer

Illegible signature

mostly irrelevant, especially when it is known that the writer must sign many letters out of professional reasons

only if other script is also illegible, it accentuates the ambiguous character of the writer

Strikingly legible

pedant

Absolute different pattern of writing in signature compared to the other script

disguise
shrewd cautiousness

Full stop and short horizontal dash behind signature

cautiousness
suspicion

All additional strokes, flourishes, over- and underlinings of the signature are to be evaluated according to their left- or right-tendency or to other features. Every such sign is a strong accentuation of the trait of character found in the other script, because the signature is the strongest demonstration and exhibition of a writer's "Ego."

XVIII. The Signs of Unreliability and Dishonesty

NB. At least four to five of the following features must appear *clearly and distinctly* in a script in order to allow a statement of any kind of dishonesty.

In a slow handwriting

1. Artificiality of the script. Stylishness

2. Covering strokes (Up- and down-strokes cover each other)

3. Partly covering strokes
    Supported strokes

    Shark-tooth

4. Arcade and slow thread

5. Rolled-in complications in initial as well as in final strokes

6. Broken letters
    Torn-off lower loops

7. Omission of letters

8. Frequent starts of the initial stroke

9. Corrections which do not increase the legibility of the script

The Signs of Unreliability
and Dishonesty

In a slow handwriting

10. Counter-strokes

    a) Middle-zone loops are open at the base

    b) Middle-zone loops have double loops

    c) Increased left-tendency especially in capitals and final strokes

    d) "a," "d," "g" and similar letters are written in two strokes

The Signs of Unreliability in a Slow Script

Artificiality of the Script

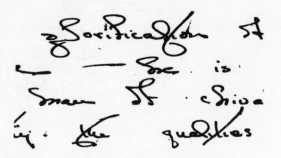

Artificial script

Stylish script

The Signs of Unreliability in a Slow Script

Covering Strokes

making machines

Down- and upstrokes cover each other on "m," "k," "h" and "n."

I meet you

Down- and upstrokes cover each other on "m" and "ou."

Yours

Down- and upstrokes cover each other on "ou" and "r."

The Signs of Unreliability in a Slow Script

Partly Covering Strokes

Up- and downstrokes partly cover each other on "u" and "m."

Up- and downstrokes partly cover each other on "u" and "n."
In the second word "days" the down- and upstrokes on "y" cover each other completely making the word almost illegible.

Shark-tooth

Partly covering up- and downstrokes on "m" and "n." These covering strokes are furthermore slightly curved resembling shark teeth.

The Signs of Unreliability in a Slow Script

Arcade and Slow Thread

How you

Marked arcade on "u"

Juan   *thens*

room.   *down.*

Left-tending final arcades on "n" and "m"

improvement over a given

something

Threadlike connections in a slow handwriting

The Signs of Unreliability in a Slow Script

Rolled-in Complications in Initial as well as in Final Strokes

Broken Letters and Torn-off Lower Loops

The letters "m," "n" and "u" are broken to pieces

The lower loops on "g" and "y" are torn off the middle-zone loops.
Additional signs: Rolled-in movements in all middle-zone loops.

186

The Signs of Unreliability in a Slow Script

Omission of Letters

actirties

The second "i" is missing in a slow script.

Frequent Starts of the Initial Stroke

What

Several starts on "W"

Great

Additional loops before starting the "G"

The Signs of Unreliability in a Slow Script

Corrections Which Do Not Increase the Legibility of the Script

[handwriting samples]

Counterstrokes

[handwriting samples]

Middle-zone loops are open on base of "b" and "o."

The Signs of Unreliability in a Slow Script

Counterstrokes

fondest

Middle-zone loops open on base of "o" and "d."
Additional sign: Arcade on "n"

of · Las · and

bad · hand · are

Middle-zone loops have double loops

Increased left-tendency especially in capitals and final strokes

Jett · Bixby

No

The Signs of Unreliability in a Slow Script

Letters Written in Two Strokes

Partition in "d"

Partition in "a"

Partition in "g"

Partitions in "a" and "d"

The Signs of Unreliability
and Dishonesty

Disregarding the speed of the script

11. Simplification of the letters to such an extent that they become ambiguous and indistinct

$$2 = \mathcal{R}$$

12. Illegibility, especially when combined with a reclining slant

13. Writing of wrong letters instead of the right ones. Genuine writing mistakes of a mature and educated writer

14. Mixed writing systems for the same letter

$$\mathcal{L} + \mathcal{E}, \quad \mathcal{r} + \mathcal{k}, \quad \mathcal{s} + s, \quad d + \partial + \delta$$

15. Marked dissimilarity of context and signature

16. Exaggerations of every kind:

   a) Exaggerated loops

   $$\mathcal{L} = \ell \qquad \mathcal{g} = g$$

   b) Exaggerated initial emphasis especially in capitals

   $$\mathcal{G} = g \qquad \mathcal{L} = \mathcal{L}$$

   c) Exaggerated and unsteady pressure

   d) Exaggerated flourishes, especially in the signature

191

The Signs of Unreliability Disregarding the Speed of the Script

Simplification of the Letters to Such an Extent that They Become Ambiguous and Indistinct

Indistinct "r"

Indistinct "W" and "r"

Indistinct "b," "g" and "e"

Illegibility, especially when Combined with a Reclining Slant

Illegible reclining script

Illegible inclining script

192

The Signs of Unreliability Disregarding the Speed of the Script

Mixed Writing Systems for the Same Letter

represent

Different "r"

encouraging

Different "g"

leisure interests

Different "s"

california

Different "a"

i conditions

delegating spor

Different "d"

little

Different "t"

Jones bad

Different "d"

every

Different "e"

The Signs of Unreliability Disregarding the Speed of the Script

Exaggerations of Every Kind

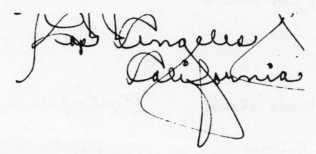

Exaggerated loops especially in the lower zone

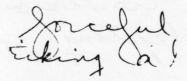

Exaggerated lower loops

Exaggerated ornamentation

The Signs of Unreliability Disregarding the Speed of the Script

Exaggerations of Every Kind

Exaggerated initial emphasis in capitals

Exaggerated pressure

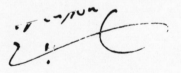

Exaggerated flourishes

Bibliography

Becker, M. *Graphologie der Kinderhandschrift*. Freiburg 1926.

Brooks, C. H. *Your Character from Your Handwriting*. London, 1946.

Bunker, M. N. *Case Book Number One*. American Institute of Graphoanalysis. Kansas City, 1936.

Crépieux-Jamin, J. *L'écriture et le caractère*. Paris, 1888.

Crépieux-Jamin, J. *Les éléments de l'écriture des canailles*. Paris, 1924.

Crépieux-Jamin, J. *ABC de la graphologie*. Paris, 1930.

Klages, L. R. *Einführung in die Psychologie der Handschrift*. Heilbronn, 1924.

Klages, L. R. *Die Grundlagen der Charakterkunde*. Ed. 6, Leipzig, 1928.

Klages, L. R. *Handschrift und Charakter*. Leipzig, 1940.

Langenbruch, M. *Praktische Menschenkenntnis auf Grund der Handschrift*, Berlin, 1929.

Lewinson, T. S. and Zubin, J. *Handwriting Analysis*: a Series of Scales for Evaluatiing the Dynamic Aspects of Handwriting. New York, 1942.

Lombroso, C. *Handbuch der Graphologie* (translation), Leipzig, 1902.

Mendel, A. O. *Personality in Handwriting*. New York, 1947.

Mendelsohn, A. and G. *Der Mensch in der Handschrift*. Leipzig, 1928.

Meyer, G. *Wissenschaftliche Grundlagen der Graphologie*. Jena, 1925.

Morf, G. *Praktische Charakterkunde*. Bern, 1945.

Pulver, M. *Symbolik der Handschrift*. Zürich, 1945.

Pulver, M. *Trieb und Verbrechen in der Handschrift*. Zürich, 1934.

Saudek, R. *The Psychology of Handwriting*. London, 1928.

Saudek, R. *Experiments with Handwriting*. London, 1928.

Schermann, R. *Die Schrift lügt nicht*. Berlin, 1929.

Schneidemühl, G. *Handschrift und Charakter*. Leipzig, 1911.

Sonnemann, U. *Handwriting Analysis*. New York, 1950.

Wolff, W. *Diagrams of the Unconscious*. New York, 1948.

INDEX

A

absolute size (of script), 30-45
abstraction, abstract thinking, 52, 136
accessory parts (of script), left- and right-tending movements in, 139-147
accuracy, 36
act of writing, 18
action, 120
active ambition, 56
activity, 33, 60, 91, 120, 178
adaptability, 60, 69, 78, 81, 84, 150, 152
additional loops, 187
additional strokes (in signatures), 179
additions (to school pattern), 172
address on envelopes, 178
adherence to old concepts, 81
adventurous, 46
aesthetic (form) sense, 25, 109, 110, 175
affectation, 66, 72, 172
affection, 60
affirmation, 69
age (of writer), 12
aggressiveness, 75, 152
agility, 111, 150

aimlessness, 104
altruism, 133
ambiguity, ambiguous, 78, 191, 192
ambition, 46, 97, 106
amiability, 139
analysis, analyst, analyze, 8, 9, 11, 12, 14-16, 94
analytical mind, 160
analytical thinking, 87
anger, 97
angles, 75-77
anti-intellectualism, 54
apathy, 25, 48
apperception, 127, 160, 163
application (of tables), 12
arcades, 72-74, 140, 145, 180, 185, 189
aridity, 58
arrogance, 15, 30, 44, 66
artificial, artificiality, 18, 21, 22, 66, 72, 180, 182
ascending steps, 102, 103
ascending straight (lines), 97, 98
asceticism, 160
assiduity, 46
authority, 146
avarice, 58, 139

B

bad taste, 172
balance, 18, 27
base (of letters), 126, 129, 130, 132, 188, 189
basic form (of letters), 172
beginning (of letters), 139, 141, 142
behavior, 66
being boring, 25
below medium (form level), 22, 23
benevolence, 69

blotted pressure, 152, 154
boastfulness, 14, 30, 163
boring, 25
braggart, 46
brainwriting, 9
broken letters, 180, 186
brutality, 152
brutal opposition, 75
bumptiousness, 44
businessmindedness, 169

C

calculation, 139
calmness, 25
capitals, 12, 13, 181, 189, 191, 195
capriciousness, 27
care, carefulness, 42, 116
carelessness, 56
catching hook, 139, 140, 143, 144
catpaw, 139, 143
caution, cautiousness, 58, 63, 72, 116, 178
character (trait), 7-12, 14, 15
characteristic, 11
chattiness, 91

chivalry, 30
circumstantiality, 172
claw-stroke, 139, 142
cleanness, 87
clear judgment, 175
clear representation of facts, 87
clearsightedness, 169
clumsiness, 54, 148
coldness, 25, 63, 75, 160
color sense, 157
comfort, 50
communicativeness, 97, 109, 110, 133

199

D

E

201

harmony, 18, 25
haste, hastiness, 56, 60, 110, 111
hastiness in drawing conclusions, 81
haughtiness, 15, 30, 44
heartiness, 165
heaven, 13
heaviness, 54, 148
height (of strokes), 25, 28, 29
hell, 13
helpfulness, 133
hermit, 84

hesitancy, 116
high pressure, 148, 149, 152-154
hooks, 125, 128, 129, 132, 139, 140, 143, 144
horizontal straight (lines), 94-96
horizontal zones, 13
hospitality, 69, 110
humility, 32
hypersensitivity, 127
hysteria, 60, 78

I

I, 10, 11, 13
id, 13
idealism, 39, 52, 155
i-dot, 20, 111, 138, 140, 145, 146, 147
illegibility, illegible (script), 175, 177, 179, 184, 191, 192
illness, 99
imagination, 46, 52, 56, 163, 169
imbecile, 84
immobility, 54
immoderateness, 60
impartiality, 42
impatience, 56, 111
imperiousness, 30
impressionability, 27, 56, 127, 155, 157
impressiveness, 60
impulses, 13, 14, 46
impulsiveness, impulsivity, 27, 91, 111, 152
inactivity, 116
inadaptability, 75
inclining (script), 192
incoherence, 87
inconsequence (in thinking), 27, 84
inconsiderateness, 33, 87
inconsistency, 84
inconstancy, 27
increase in concentration, 136
increase (in movement, tendency), 120, 181, 189
indecision, 27
independence, 14, 33, 84, 178,
independence of judgment, 84
indetermination, 69
indifference, 25, 48, 63
indistinct, 191, 192
individual consciousness, 17
individualism, 84
individuality, 9
indolence, 48, 116
inertia, 116
inferiority feelings, 32
influence of the past, 178
informality, 109

inhibition, 13, 58, 140, 178
initial emphasis, 191, 195
initial formality, 109
initial shyness, 110
initial strokes, 180, 186, 187,
initial upstrokes, 139, 141
initiative, 60, 81, 84, 111, 150
ink, 12
ink-filled (loops), 157, 159
inner conflicts, 39
inner difficulties, 13
inner life, 120
inner resources, 169
inner security, 25
inner values, 50
insincerity, 72, 78, 116, 140, 172, 175
instability, 69, 91, 111
instinct, 14, 17
instinctive apperception of the past, 127
instinctive contact to the environment, 178
instinctive inhibitions, 178
instinctive understanding, 136
instinctual thinking, 91
intellectual approach, 130
intellectual initiative, 84
intellectual self-centredness, 131
intellectual self-defense, 139
intellectual self-dependence, 121
intellectual thoughts, 14, 17
intelligence, 52, 78, 81
interest, 46, 63, 110
interpretation (of script, of character), 7, 8
introversion, 13, 17, 58, 116, 120
intuition, intuitive thinking, 16, 84
inventiveness, 84
inversion of the libido, 127
inverted loop, 126
irregularity, irregular script, 15, 25-29, 152-156
irresolution, 27, 69, 116
irritability, 27, 111, 152, 169
isolation, 87, 110, 120

202

J

jealousy, 58
join, desire to, 133

judgment, 130
jumpiness, 84

K

kindness, 69, 110

L

lability, 155
lack of apperception, 160
lack of balance, 27
lack of care, 39
lack of concentration, 33, 46
lack of confidence in future, 178
lack of conscience, 78
lack of determination, 150
lack of differentiation, 148
lack of direction, 27
lack of discipline, 56
lack of elasticity, 42
lack of emotion, 63, 94
lack of energy, 150
lack of enthusiasm, 42
lack of forethought, 84
lack of form sense, 109, 169, 175
lack of frankness, 72
lack of imagination, 169
lack of initiative, 81, 150
lack of interest, 63
lack of observation, 27
lack of purpose, 27
lack of reserve, 56, 110
lack of resistance, 150
lack of restraint, 60
lack of roots, 52
lack of self-confidence, 32
lack of self-control, 56
lack of self-criticism, 163
lack of sense of reality, 39
lack of sensuality, 160
lack of spirituality, 157
lack of spontaneity, 87
lack of sympathy, 75
lack of taste, 110

lack of vivacity, 94
lack of will power, 99
large (script), 15, 179
lavishness, 87, 109
laziness, 69, 116
leadership, 33, 44, 120
leanness (of letters), 169-171
left margin, 109
left (side), 13, 14. 17, 127, 137, 140. 145
left-tendency, left-tending movements, 14, 119-129, 131, 137-145, 179, 181, 185, 189
leftward slant, 66-68
legibility, legible, 18-20, 172, 179, 180, 188
letter (forms), 10-13, 18, 19, 163-177
libido, 127
lines, 12-14, 94-108
liveliness of interests and impulses, 46
loftiness, 155
logic, 81
loneliness, 84
long-term planning, 33
looped letters, 163
loops, 121-132, 134, 136-138, 157, 180, 181, 186, 188, 189, 191, 194
loquacity, 97
love of independence, 178
lower loops, 126, 127, 132, 157, 180, 186, 194
lower margin, 109
lower zone, 13, 14, 46-52, 54, 55, 119, 122, 123, 126-129, 134, 136-138, 143, 159, 167-169, 171, 194
low pressure, 150, 151, 155, 156
lyrical inclination, 121

M

male, 12
malice, 58, 160
mannerism, 72
margins, 109, 110
masculinity, 148
materialism, materialistic (impulses), 17, 54, 157, 169
materialistic and instinctive contact to the environment, 178

materialistic or instinctive inhibitions, 178
matter-mindedness, 54
matter-of-factness, 42, 169, 175
maturity, 14, 18, 22, 175
meaning (of trait), 12, 14, 15, 17, 120
meditation, meditativeness. 120, 121
medium form level, 15, 22, 23
medium speed, 114, 115

203

N

O

P

204

205

T

U

207